Beyond the Blackbird Field

Also by Adèle Ogiér Jones and published by Ginninderra Press

Poetry

Afghanistan – waiting for the bus
From the Edge of the Pacific
Sense of Place (Pocket Poets)

Fiction

Desert Diya

Adèle Ogiér Jones

Beyond the Blackbird Field

Beyond the Blackbird Field
ISBN 978 1 76041 192 3
Copyright © text Adèle Ogiér Jones 2016
Cover photograph from Pixabay (CC0 Public Domain)

First published 2016 by
GINNINDERRA PRESS
PO Box 3461 Port Adelaide 5015 Australia
www.ginninderrapress.com.au

Contents

Sunset	9
Pristina sunset	11
Kosovo horizon	12
For sun going down	13
Sunflowers in the Balkans	14
Borders	15
Drummer boy	16
Storyteller	18
Shadërvani fountain	19
Wild cherry plums	20
Boys on the square	21
Figurine beyond glass	22
The weaving store	23
For the old hammam	24
Artists on the road	25
Vignette	26
Dragon mountain	27
Kosovo tulips	28
The garden	29
Sunset words	30
Fire beans	31
Supermarket at sunset	32
Evening	33
Hemingway in Prizren	35
Sounds in the hammam	36
Travellers	38
Prizren laneway	40
Windfalls	41
Apron stains	42

Weaving	43
Cellist	44
Evening fog	45
Limun	46
Postcard	47
Terracotta goddess	48
Sounds	49
Ensemble	50
For Parvin	52
Insight	53
Sharing the bowl	54

Night — 55

Beyond the blackbird field	57
Grapevines on the road to Prizren	58
Midnight	60
That hour called night	61
Moon's daughter	62
Nightshift	63
Words to a moon	64
Fancy dress	65
New things	67
Film crew	68
Nectar	69
Fox	70
Moonlight	71
Birds in snow	72
Bazaar	73
Harmonica song	74
Autumn's first night	76
Sepia	77

Dubrovnik	79
Towards dawn	81
Fishing boats	82
Daybreak on Dubrovnik	83
Smoke	85
Dawn in the old city	86
Fleeting images	87
Dawn haiku	88
Mostar	89
Sunset on Mostar	91
Evening	92
Night	93
Daybreak	94

Sunset

cool sinks down after
heatwave drained streets fall lifeless
where cornflowers smiled

Pristina sunset

The wonderful thing about sunsets
even on the bleakest day
at the darkest moment
in the greyest environment,
they are there
unstoppable
shouting out
without words.

Kosovo horizon

newfound
perspective
as two paths meet
east and west converging
far beyond the sunset
where sky meets the horizon
green skirts ringing grey-blue mountains
while forgotten vineyards smile sadly, looking in
gazing from a valley's resounding silence
where bloodied shoots break through winter earth
promising beauty for new lovers
gathering in spring time
old enmity overcome
friendship replacing
bleak memories
connecting
evening
dreams

For sun going down

slowly sunset sings
against the purple backdrop
of my weeping heart

palest winter sun
sinks graciously in curtsey
before grand evening

fleeting winter sun
gathers raindrops running
silver overhead

Sunflowers in the Balkans

In the depth of winter greyness
bare vines grown old with the weight of age
forgotten for as long as young minds can remember
seen only in memories of old men and women
collecting their fruit
to press juices together
with laughter and song
knowing that joy awaits them.

Without sunflowers to brighten and gladden
a landscape denuded of colour and change
deep sadness grips spirits puzzling cold
waiting for another touch
to welcome summer to their land
golden beams through froth clouds
matched by the strange joy
of brilliant sunflowers gleefully proud.

Sunflowers in the Balkans
calling out to each other
in merriment, forgetting grey
lost in the moment of another season
a language speaking
words unheard in solemn winter
forgetting the loveliness of hearts
reflecting the glow of sun on the land.

Borders

Children crossing on solemn journeys
searching work or markets for goods of little worth
see no border marking this place on the ground
no soil of different hue and colour
only posts with words they cannot read
and uniforms proclaiming ownership.

Speaking dialects and tongues
of neighbours through villages and towns
crossing appears the natural thing to do
without a post prohibiting, preventing
journeys their fathers and those before them made
no hesitation or attention to what officials declared
like seeds of sunflowers
blown in the wind, warmed only by sun.

As bees touch down for single songs
flying off to find new nectar sweet at sunset
children see no sense to halt at borders
except to escape the frown and rule imposed
deportation to where their language is most known
though they speak them all with ease.

Children crossing on weary trekking
families resting on their backs
school experiences the day provides
learning keeps them strong for days to come
no need of borders imposed outside them
no danger greater than family loss
waiting, expecting sons to join their fathers
lost to other lands, ground which claimed them long before.

Drummer boy

There is little to be told
from the old photo of a boy,
now creased and cracked,
where he still stands proud
shoulders hunched just slightly
from the weight of the drum he holds.

A Kosovo photo long ago
in a village near a school
old stone walls crumbling,
the single chance a better way,
four boys look on smiling
proud as drumming echoes flow.

Taqiyah cap frames glowing eyes
the smile, still strong teeth
though here is little to dream about
as life goes on and each one strives
hands cracked, backs stooped from farming
land bearing crops which barely survive.

The drumming makes the memory
of childhood sweet and strong
though there is little in the cold
to justify this reverie
a past made up by grateful men
to cover war's catastrophes.

Drumming for the weddings
and leading men to war
another side to drummer boys
trudging oozing mud, dreading
scattered bodies lying in the snow
like untouched roses on virgin beds.

The drummer boy is old now
or maybe he has gone,
photos forming memories
in a calm, uneasy peace
with youth in war forgotten
if men's nightmares and their pacts allow.

Storyteller

Storytelling over
the old man leans back reflecting
watching worlds go by
watching rivers twist beneath bridges
just as they always have done
watching clouds gather and float
sadness and heaviness
brimming over
bringing relief
and then
new stories.

Shadërvani fountain

Drinking from the fountain in Pristina
behind the Çarshia mosque
means coming back
and still today the tasting
signifies returning.

Legend says it over
and old men smoking
near the fountain
repeat the story,
fate older than its telling.

Behind the market mosque
for travellers passing through
resting after work and prayer
water free to drink
fountain's hospitality.

Sweetness for the taking
with bitterness around forgotten,
symbol of old days
when animosity
cowered, and springs refreshed.

Myths live on in old men's tales
in Pristina where gracious ease
lives again after the pain,
hospitality springing forth
like the fountain in the square.

Wild cherry plums

Growing wild in a corner of an evening garden
neglected by those too busy to bother with a single tree,
tiny tart cherry plums
slightly withered even before falling
too tired on their branches to grow plump
hardly enough juice or flesh for the brewing
wrong variety
like so much left standing, like those remaining
too many gone to find better prospects in a peacetime
offering little compensation.

Further down the road dusty at day's end
children are squealing throwing pebbles of dried plums
for others to catch,
slightly worried women call out
too tired to rebuke them with fathers gone
hardly surviving, searching for work
little chance now
for this country at peace, mothers remaining
finding work where they can, make brandy and jam
remaining plums their chance to survive.

Women call out to the children at play
to leave alone cherry plums to be shared by them all
soft complaining murmurs
as they go about their gathering, reaping the remaining
before their meal, almost too small to be noticed
cherry plums changing from sour to sweet
their time is ripe,
children growing wild like the little plums they gather
will remember these days long after the summer trees
have withered away.

Boys on the square

Uneasy truce with lads on the edge
of the square near dusk
accepted because they must be,
rights and dignity and a declaration demands
determining justice for child workers
youth forgotten
too early with experiences beyond their years
deported from countries to the west,
waiting for another chance to enter
though not wanted,
nowhere home for nowhere calls as place
to lay their heads for ever,
never belonging and having not for centuries,
loitering without intent
lingering with hopes
that there will be something
in keeping with their longing
for freedom,
and the search
beyond this night.

Figurine beyond glass

Determining still the place and the time
she stands firm
leaning to one side
knuckles steadily on hips
broad for children she will bear
eyes staring blankly to the earth, sightless
yet seeing more than those who walk it,
face fixed, disclosing little
except her place and role
continuing creation
proclaiming that she and her kind will decide
for she rules fertility.

Nose like a bird swooping on the terrain below
choosing whatever she sees as her delicacy
beak for the women of earth and beyond
sightless eyes gazing deep into the heart
beyond roles she declares are fantasy
forgotten in time
erect on the podium, her throne
the earth this night,
discovered anew
displayed for sceptics to research
the art of a moon goddess behind glass
intoxicating, stealing each heart,
reason besieged as she entices afresh
just as she always has done.

The weaving store

Two women stand behind a bench
serving at a counter
puzzled, disinterested
or faintly suspicious of the afternoon intruder in their store,
no customers, no tourists enter here
where there is no sign.

Men in the laneway slow to indicate
where few have entered for many years
since observers and peacekeepers left,
family weaving no longer prized far away
where rugs, cloth and brass from new troubled lands
become today's fashion.

Weaving of women hardly noticed
in a Kosovo seldom heard on travellers' lips
now there is quiet once more,
old weaving continues as it always has
for old women treasuring memories
of skills and art long gone.

The women hesitate beyond the barrier
separating them from unfamiliar customs and words
defence no longer needed
yet reticent as something unspoken remains
fearing, for strangers never enter their lanes
where there are no signs to show the way.

For the old hammam

shared water gone now
forgotten memories of war
stone beauty remains

welcoming hands closed
sunsets forgotten in war
hamman's warmth, cold stone

conqueror's beauty
closed to outsiders, standing firm
speaking war's ugliness

Artists on the road

Caravan parked on the curb
behind the trailer van blocking the view
the one the locals have complained about for years
threatening to report its illegality
though the number plate gives it status
a child of the city
standing out in defiance
of tidy minds, would-be artists.

Artists on the road
sprawled across the sides and the rear
blue flag with circlet of stars, commands respect
though golden yellow slightly tarnished
mirroring dandelions of the field
where sheep graze late
oblivious to the significance
of lives on four wheels on the verge of the field.

Vignette

i

As daytime heat dies with the sun
a breeze
remarkable in its coolness emerges,
long hidden in caves
waiting for the dark
to invite stars on a clear, black night
waiting to blow a gentle tune
through rustling leaves.

ii

Red roses on dry earth
crumbling clay
sunset surprises
in a land spilled with blood,
blooming pink and red and mauve
reflecting mountains
embracing villages at dusk
one with the sinking sun.

Dragon mountain

Dragon mountain
weeping tears
with waters which heal
desperate spirits,

red spine opened wide
by a knights' protecting sword
crevice so deep
that minds feel fear,

pink ripples like ferns
pale ochre and white
magically healing
those who believe.

Kosovo tulips

Tulips no longer foreign here
small and open to receive the phallus of spring,
deep multicoloured
dark with the mystery of night
dark red-purple as the deepest shiraz
dark as the blood of a slow seeping wound
lightly fragranced
deeply hued.

Tulips and irises
purple meeting mauve to reflect the lilac sprays
subtle and perfumed
soft with the memory of love
intoxicating, erotic as the longest night of love
perfume brimming over, overwhelming taste and flavour
evoking gentle memories
deeply formed.

Red variegated
in the foreground like highlights of memory,
regal with noble purples
pinks hint at fun
while crimson blood stocks, simple, old fashioned
stand the test of time
reflected in water
centennials en masse.

The garden

A splash of colour in all of this is the bed of orange tulips
standing as onlookers by the pond,
streaming old-fashioned hues, tulips, stocks and pansies
rude, obnoxious and irreverent in this garden,
more than a gaudy colour splash
standing together crowded
uninvited to the ceremony
making a spectacle of themselves anyway.

If the red is the blood of a cross this Easter
the purples are bitter aloes
or cloaks of the hierarchy,
governments making judgments
for the people rendered speechless,
choices lost amidst background noise.

Yet orange tulips promise a stage beyond this platform
hope which does not get caught up in all of this,
untouched by the drama
forgotten by history
but definite, a spectacle
at this point in time.

Sunset words

How can one write of the beauty of autumn
or speak of the pain of love
beauty and pain
sweetness and torment
radiant gold proclaiming day's end
despair when gone?

Artists attempting colour, tempting light
autumn on canvas far from the truth
words unable to grasp
or convey the moment
when ecstasy subsides,

beauty on cursed mountains
passion written in pain
ache for the loss
while memory lives on.

Fire beans

Tecoma grows bold along a sunset railing
reminding me of home
where it wandered wilder in the sun
across a fence bent over with the weight
of orange and vermilion blooms
silent as a flame
wildly spreading out of control
belonging forever on broken down fences
transported to driest of towns
and in Victoria another,
these persistent flowers
still open after sunset.

Supermarket at sunset

Open at sunset after evening prayer
remarkable
in unchanging dress
standing still for a while
at Kosovar Road's end,
time capsule delivered from another era.

New Chinese side by side now
with the regulation American fast food joint
unchanged save for shops selling
new ethnic dress remembering the old
embroidered with colour
in place of the gold.

Near the outdoor diner
a woman wandering alone,
night invitations a shock, unexpected
where still solid reputation is norm,
making the solitary bookstore invitation
delightful.

Metropolis in blocks of a market,
stores confined
as never were stalls of farmer's and bazaar men
could or would want to be
near the old supermarket
crowded out on the corner of the block.

Evening

storytelling ends
evening swathes aged oceans
whispering new songs

Hemingway in Prizren

In stories of his travels there is no mention
of Hemingway in Prizren
though he passed on his Balkan journey
aboard the train
headed for Istanbul,
so perhaps he diverged
unrecorded, a love untold,
a story beckoning him deeper
into the heart of the Balkans
memories murmured in later years,
divulged to none
except the keeper of songs
from the heart
the deepest recesses
where stories are gathered and fanned out
in the evening of creative life
or perhaps he saw the river
babbling its tale through the town
near the roadside in Prizren
by the café they named after him.

Sounds in the hammam

Hiss of steam
water on smouldering charcoal
slapping wet cloth
on bodies worn from work and life
water splashing
from fountains and faucets
jugs and taps
in pools and underground cisterns hidden from sight.

Echoes of voices
solitary and alone in a place of refreshment
calling to attendants
more water, oil, cloths and mantles
easing daily burdens
calm reverberating
from friends and old neighbours
villagers and travellers all one.

Communal gathering place
on the edge of the square
hammam near a church and the mosque
each inviting its own
to calm spirits, cleanse minds,
feet flopping in sandals and shoes
worn down at the heel still caked in mud
from the fields and the laneways and the dust of the town.

Greetings of thanks as they stream their way out
farewell to attendants
and to the travellers salaam
as they join in the prayer
and afterwards the meal
in homes, caravanserais or inns
animosities forgotten, forgiven
this day, an aftermath of bathing as one.

The hammam again tells stories
whispered in warm alcoves
repeated in voices raised with laughter
nodding heads listening in silence
soft mutterings
from the guests well used to its customs and ease
wood water heater stoking gossip
exchanged as evening wears on.

Travellers

These streets have seen travellers
have felt the steps of its children
heard the roar of armies
and invaders passing through
some staying longer
setting up or imposing
new laws and rulers
each with their own regulations
reformed taxes and duties
new music, religion, and speech.

These streets have felt wheels
of the wagons, carts and trucks
of each passing wave
with their intentions to stay
changing older accepted ways
replacing yesterday's governors,
directing in new garb
deciding anew for today's people
change has become constant
in this land of past memories.

These streets could tell stories
of invasion and displacement
of refugees from war lost
in the babble repeated
journalists and reporters interpret
each family's sorrows
few untouched, most hiding
the depth of their tragedy
neighbours became enemies
through dictates of politics and revolt.

These streets know peaceful times
regularity and calm
as people trudge on
with the business of living
coming and going to markets and schools
marrying and burying
these streets carry them all
through life's days together
as streets are remade, resealed
more dreams and fresh dancing.

Sweet song of nightingale's evening
well after dark
when other sounds and commotion close down,
or of frogs far too delicate to find
for crickets cannot sing such tunes
too late for summer cicadas,
songbirds and peacocks hidden beyond fences
in the darkness of night
their sad songs for our dreaming
peace beyond crumbling concreted walls.

Prizren laneway

Dull shadows of lace
no light left to brighten the path
along the alleyway neglected, grimy
a naked bulb hangs
distraught
choked by wires crisscrossing overhead
stolen lines
saving meters of neighbours,
elegant laneway at the head of the alley
lies reminiscing its romantic past
which did not exist
except in the minds of dreamers.

Iron lampshades twirling and coiling
weaving in and out and around
like moths playing
on this warm summer's night
forgotten by all save the few who live down here,
wary travellers seeking permission
as day ends its watch,
streets in the town still alive with the music
locked away from these lanes
and the silence of alleys
closed to all
heedless of time.

Windfalls

Yesterday I collected evening windfalls
apples sweet and a little bruised
ready to be tasted
more delightful than taking others not quite ripe
predictably waiting to be selected
plucked for their firmness
and early promises.

Apron stains

Who was the woman
with yesterday's apron stains
long before woven?

Where is the woman
her attire covered over
culture's signature?

Where sings the woman
who donned this relic
long before treasured with pride?

Weaving

Weaving rare for most today
yet sometimes
old Kosovo art
carried and copied from neighbours,
found searching in back streets
where the devoted
can see and touch apron cloth
made the old way
by hand
red white patterns twined
roughly together
like people of old.

Cellist

On the furthest step to the right of the friary entrance
a lone musician stoops to fix the stand where his music will rest,
the same each day at sunset, just before the passing procession
through laneways announcing the end of day
as travellers head out to the guesthouses and inns
where they rest for the night.

Never disturbed by the friars within
perhaps an arrangement as the music
calms their tension
wondering what has become of their lives
glad that again they are free to move and pray
as they like, where they will.

Music repeated evening after evening
sometimes a variation of order but set pieces
an expected repertoire
predictability and sameness colliding
with a peace, for what is expected
takes place.

Sweetly and sure, confident, contained
eyes closed to any who choose to stop, to observe
to listen to his music
taking them to other times
or transporting them to the beauty
of the moment,

as airs float on the cool evening breeze
murmuring across the square
soothing at the end of the day.

Evening fog

Stalking stealthily, creeping
behind and between
fog wrapped around naked pines
capturing silence,
mist laced around fingers and branches
locking unspoken words fast
holding onto our secrets,
soft spoken poems transcribed on butterflies' wings
gossamer too fine to touch
gliding memories
warm in the late evening silence
held fast by strict sentinels
guarding our hearts like the rigid pines
all around,
with late afternoon rays
now blocked by clouds descending
and the grey fog of nightfall
forbidding
enticing
protecting this passing moment.

Limun

After the chai khana has closed and urns turned down
for the evening
teas and coffees from far away sealed firmly
away from the damp
which will spoil them for the following day,
another treasure is uncovered in homes of friends
gathering to share the warmest moments
before nightfall is firmly announced,
limun
from fruits coloured by sunlight
shaded like sunlight
tasting like sunlight
on the sourest of nights
in the dark,
limun
lemon's elixir seems common
ordinary and simply produced
yet women and their men compete to make it
sweeter and tarter than neighbours'
magical gold secreted away
guarded with pride
glistening in lamp light
at evening, for friendship
after the bitterest of days,
on the sweetest of evenings with their promise.

Postcard

Words never read
from the grey cell of your mind
gazing at the window and through it
perhaps not seeing the ferns nodding into the bare room
green bouncing on white walls
stark, sterile, no bacteria, no life
yours ever low
your thoughts somewhere else
you cannot explain the memories
and stories,
point to the people we cannot see
speaking
spirits beyond our recognition
hidden except to one such as you
moving beyond twilight and dawn
into a forest of your own making
perhaps where a solitary sunflower blooms
a tiny red ladybird resting there
peacefully
contrasting these signs of hope
beyond our knowing
your bed slowly becoming a riverbank
cool, distracting.

Terracotta goddess

Once she was fulcrum of the year,
revolving seasons
life and birth
fruitfulness and plenty
fertility's pivot planted wide
in hearts of all who toiled,
hope for barren fields and wombs
dry or frozen with juices trapped below
a goddess
fashioned from the clay,

giving warmth on cold evenings,
comfort when none
could be found
in the dark mystery
endearing charms still hidden deep,
companion for the women
fecund and bountiful
touch alone releasing life's sweet
liquid this Eve
created from clay.

Sounds

Music turned up loud in a room nearby
to drown out the megaphone of prayer
a rasping song, forties music and a cricket
chirping loudly above, in syncopated rhythm
a modern symphony, an ancient collision
and the dogs bark, adding one more voice.

One by one, singly then in competition
the sounds of this night in opposition yet combining
into a harmony of sound and invasion
one on top of the other, only the insect original
a cacophony of sound, blending and harmonizing
could Stockhausen have done better?

Like instruments in opposition, apposition, one more note
as a car roars past on the quiet evening road
the breeze lifts the praying voice in waves
a memory of the past, echoing on the night
a wind rustles leaves, another distant voice
raised in prayer, bemoaning the day.

The praying stops, barking ends and the crickets,
as if understanding, cease their song
until finally all that is left is the sound
of the breeze and the rustling leaves
whispering softly
singing silver tongued
to the night
soft at last quiet peaceful and dark.

Ensemble

A single string of the çiftelia sounds beautiful here
a guitar and accordion can bring a listener to ecstasy
a long trip, short preparations then a performance
like a bud transforming to full bloom, full eroticism.

A stage set for dual musicians, guitar and accordion
at their feet lodra and mandolin wait for the moment
a slight cadence, gently building, swelling to roundness
like a spark bursting into full flame, full heat.

The accordion whispers, one note then and beautiful on the air
fingers moving down, down and across a bridge, ivory on black
then full throated and singing in deepest melodies
rich, exuberant, romantic, assured.

On and on with the guitar in ascendance and then falling
as the accordion dominates, each playing to the other
making love, aching for control, sensitive
to the improvisations of the other, each time new.

Then to the stage robed players stroll, ancient and regal
red flowers presented in expectation of what is to come,
scarlet cushion reflecting the crimson of the accordion
as it weaves wide, then closes, spreading and collapsing.

Single displays, applause and joined by its ancient mate
in new ways, unheard before, unknown contortions
together and alone, then another and the fourth, each
its own musician aware of the other, enjoying the rhythm.

In unison, in opposition, each enjoying the feeling
exhilarated by the sound which was not the same as yesterday
new sounds with old, ancient rhythm and melodies
cadences unknown to each other, intervals newly felt and heard.

Building to a crescendo unheard in traditional houses
novel experiments in Paris and Marseille transposed
an audience cheering in as many languages as instruments themselves
encore to guitar and lodra, accordion and mandolin, old and
strange together.

For Parvin

I hear butterflies knocking at my window
where fog sinks thick and sweet
near fields which look to autumn
as I remember another singer,
the poet with her butterfly wings
refusing capture
rejecting all
conventions
bent on surmounting her
like others
dried, mounted
and pinned
to a wall display,
a road named after her in the capital
of the land which ignores
butterflies
fluttering in the early dark of the evening.

Insight

Eyes deep enough to water a land
thirsty from drought decades,

eyes dark with shadow known only in darkness
shadow from rock
sharp mountain ridges,

eyes defined deeper and blacker and wild
with kohl or kajal from the holiest land,
staring deeply, intensely and long
piercing, awakening a primitive need,

eyes highlighted further with tribal attire
turbaned beard and cheeks burned from sun,
from another time, ancient, unknown
far from cities, from media and war,

eyes reflecting prophetic fervour
rejecting, desiring eyes too exposed,
striking a shiver of shame's recognition
tradition far from town streets,

eyes gazing in wonder
still fill with dread
the vulnerable, new self-assured,

eyes closed in calm weariness at day's end
reflecting life's strangeness.

Sharing the bowl

Our father talked of Albanians he worked with
picking fruit from orchards
on farms
in the years of Depression,
good blokes, friendly and quiet.

He always spoke fondly
of the custom he found strange
yet liked,
food from the bowl
placed in the centre of the circle
on the table or ground
placed on a rug to keep it clean
for they shared it always.

When it came to the meal
all welcome to join,
our fathers too,
the Depression's evening repast,
survival for all.

Night

fog lapping lame legs
of pine trees lost to night's mist
demanding service

Beyond the blackbird field

The owl calls out through a silent dark night
A faint echo sounds back down the hillside
Tired listening to dreams till earliest light
Spent summoning loves destiny denied.

They sang in the fields when all was despair
The dark kept them calm in closed hamlet huts
Hospitality found in foxes' lairs
Shots rang out twisting and wrenching men's guts.

Beyond the blackbird field, Kosovo peace
In gardens neglected new sprouting shoots
In families surviving, sense of relief
As stories retold go back to old roots.

As snow clothes with silence the warring crowds
In Kosovo's spring, new harmonies allowed.

Grapevines on the road to Prizren

Grapevines abandoned
lie still and quiet
neglected and alone
forgotten and forgetting
the years of laughter and pleasure,
reaping, pressing, dancing
and celebration for the new wine
wine for the tables of country folk.

Twisted dark against the sky
now sprouting forth their hopeful leaves
in a new spring and summer,
fruits gathered reluctantly
as imported crops are cheaper
market sellers rejecting
slighter, duller, unattractive
jewels beside the lush imports.

Webs from earth surviving
sprouting each new year in hope
that a day will come again
that day which celebrates and sings
as different languages and faces
join hands, rub shoulders
their common aim and single view
harmony in simply living.

Memory's vines withstanding
those guns and shelling
neglected months as labouring farmers
were taken or took others,
grape vines ignored,
unheeded, though if they could tell
these too would have their stories
other than wine and merrymaking.

Old roman vines imported
withstanding snow, enduring smoke
of war and its antagonism,
grapes simply budding then withering
once for eating
lost the stamping joyful dancing
crushing midst the village laughter
abandoned now till dreams awake.

Midnight

Too late
for curfew's warning
to a guesthouse known only to few,
silence
though a sense of eyes watching
as cold bites
in the sad dismal light
of a naked bulb from a shadowy past,
too late to backtrack
without creating attention
security ignored
on a distracted night
silence screeching
its sodden warning
for damp footsteps escaping
the eeriness of midnight
oozing invisibly down alleyways
lingering at dark corners
luring innocent wanderers into forgotten pasts.

That hour called night

Purple is the sour taste in a dry mouth
frozen in hours too early to be called morning,
twisted tastes
cardboard frowns
grimaces of pain
tasting broken dreams
unripe and never to bloom
evening's promises of fruitfulness
bitter hard green
fruit promising gold
red and magenta, violet
washed away in dull purple
the end of the day before tomorrow's maybe.

Moon's daughter

The house was filled with sweetest flowers the night you came,
wild and fragrant with a promise that all would change
the heaviness of male feet tramping
regardless of the atmosphere which loomed,
your coming sweet fulfilment
a dream which seemed not true
but we rejoiced
and others with us smelling violets and heather
and other blossoms from a land so far away,
the promise of forget-me-nots in winter
of pansies and perfumes to comfort
a heavy house
those darkest nights,
you brought us flowers
though you never knew.

Nightshift

When the sky changes from black to deep grey
silhouetting the lines of the mountainside on the far edges
of time
night firmly entrenched for an hour or two
though clouds have other thoughts
shabby and thin
blocking stars against the lightening sky
nothing dramatic enough to make them remarkable,
a car in the distance
too early for trains or the trams of the city
late enough for shift workers returning
and early travellers off to the unknown,
too early for rising
without the dawn song to welcome
the time when the soul overwhelms the body of thought
perplexing,
then the promised new day
different from the last
and the days before that
perhaps this day will be different
another voice, a different face
a vacant gaze from lonely travellers
the ones we met the night before
in our dreams.

Fancy dress

Dissatisfied with the attire she wears this night,
a winter moon changes and gazes at her reflection on earth far below
first one, glamorous, remarkable for the brilliance
then as if this is too much for the moon gazer
the overreaction
covering bare flesh
with the gauze of mist's coloured chiffon.

Fog passing by soft grey dove wings turning to blue
matching the hour after midnight
floating across the white body
this veil of one hundred and one thousand nights
hiding form, tempting like the dance
smiling for the minds craving
release from the dry years of emptiness.

Seven veils, then a cloak, holding all, hiding more,
the knowing, fire in the belly
waiting as it slowly performs its strip tease
a corner at first
the taste licking lips
twisting, weaving
so more can be seen.

Hidden again, nothing revealed
then as if the lone dancer will be snatched any moment
the dread which catches the sky
lighting up slowly to hide the temptation,
slow solo dance overtaken by other lights
dissatisfied with attention
devotion shown to this single danseuse,

Lights in the windows across the hillside
soft morning light of the grey winter sky
dark clouds settling now on the extrovert moon
performance soon over the audience bereft,
no satisfaction, no scintillation
tomorrow another night as fantasy and coveting waits.

Words to a moon

Watching the moon lurks
behind floating clouds teasing
eagerness aroused

knowing the moon hides
hidden in darkness mocking
anticipation

calm moonlight fingers
beckoning restless sleepers
focused on dreaming

slowly deepening
sensuous moon beckoning
luxurious liquid orb

focused on dancing
clouds spar with the winter moon
glowing serenade

New things

There is something very new when the snow is softly falling
and the world around is dark,
when the lights from across the hill
shine dimly
like the eyes of cats
waiting for the barn's provision
of mice which keep them there
with other little creatures only known to winter,
no sound from falling flakes
no raindrops on rooves
smattering against the window slightly ajar
only the clock beating the hour
persistent
more demanding than the snow.

Film crew

Three of them came like magi
following their dream, stars
emblazoned
no gold, frankincense or myrrh
though these would have been easier to carry
than magic treasure chests, filled with music and light.

Dreams drove them
No dreams of security, military, finance
but capturing hope in people
willing to go on through the dark
travelling life's roads less whole than they started
yet unbroken.

Searching for angles to share
reason and meaning, the alchemist's secret
not metal to gold but tragedy to hope
negatives transformed by light
in the darkness of despair
the will to love again in the night.

Nectar

I captured your eyes in the dark hills at night
long before the stars had faded
to pale dawn, tentative
no word spoken
meeting as if for the first time
singing in a land where love songs and poems were tradition
and wine for the soul
forbidden expression
allusion
illusion when all around was so harsh
love lost in loneliness
longing for the music
silenced
loveliness sweet as nectar
honey from wild bees on the caves
in the hills
near a place almost forgotten in time.

Fox

Too early to be morning
though far beyond the night
a lone fox wanders outside
pine nut brown in the moonlight
leaving footprints
light in the snow
gone by morning if another fall visits
frozen hard overlooked by all except those searching.

In the moonlight
patrolling from house to house
unsure of the catch
seeking what has been lost or forgotten
in farmers' memories
a single fox
alone in the snow,
lonely in the morning
before daybreak,
the last left alone in the world
as the church clock strikes five times
in the darkness over the silent field.

Moonlight

Moonlight streaming, changing the room
reflected by clouds dressed in silver sequined chiffon,
then a moment of cloudburst
struggling through the light,
no offering of fire to warm
frozen eyes gazing up
no waxing and waning
of this moon in winter this night
or those after it,
hidden behind clouds
emerging fully grown with its breasts of crystal light
shimmering
on trees whitened
like naked skeletons against the dark winter's sky,
calm spectres, resigned, peaceful
holding back the heavens rumbling in the distance,
this treasure
perfect
this globe
winking
enticing
drawing my soul nearer and nearer.

Birds in snow

Sparrows scratching in the garden box
covered with last night's snow
waiting futile
hoping they will find the birdhouse set below
blackbirds curious hover
in the tree close by
unseduced
more intent on
taming nature
breaking all boundaries
closer to the sky
while snow settles softly
then solid in the cold
lying unclaimed
piling higher
as dawn blankets further
freezing
as ice takes hold.

Bazaar

Debating the actions of history
stories retold and handed on through the night
by generations of storytellers
at the bazaar on the frontier
changing hands with fresh money over tea,
entangled and delicate their telling.

Seldom are cobwebs woven more finely
multiple reworking blurring older shape and form,
dead spiders captured
in webs of their making
in the grand bazaar
in tales through the night.

Harmonica song

Media news cannot capture
what it meant to be together in the rush
and turmoil and near anarchy never knowing
what was next, safety and security preoccupying
minds and conversations of visiting workers, keepers of peace
makers of peace, commentators on war and terror
survival preoccupying minds, daily work and dreams
of families struggling with little sense of future.

I shall come back to hear your songs
and tunes, your melodies and rhythms in my ears
harmonica melody simple, sure
rhythm of early morning blackbirds beating
tunes of far away, arid, desperate lands
small happiness and brief respite on sojourns
songs not be repeated in hearts outside the history
of this land's stories, so long, so sad.

Media reports bleak, little hope beyond tomorrow
narrow paths in lands where hope is lost
faith in better tomorrows left lying on the ground
seeds watered with dreams of longing, expected blossoming
while animosity beats hearts' doors, breaking seclusion
an inner curtain saves souls, the will to love again
strength that trusts enough to see in eyes
weariness, the cry for life without discord, harmony.

In the depths of night
dreams of long ago, of strength and valour
beauty, poetry and song, sung from mouths
of women without men, rising from the dust, from golden fountains
when further to the west, other troubadours roamed with song
beauty in their words, these poet philosophers
with their love of life, their songs of romance for the soul
their songs of beauty and the beloved.

Your poems were hidden then, hidden in history's dust
unfitting for fighters toughened, invasion repeated
called in names of armies, insurgencies, new governments
treated warily, with suspicion, old poems feared
but songs live on in evening hearts, in minds which hear the beat
the rhythm pounding, tunes invading minds at rest on darkest nights
wishing to forget the miseries of past
eased with songs of love, sunset's chorus and times of peace.

Autumn's first night

Water sings louder
in the heart of night's darkness
rushing to nowhere,
water runs gaily
alone in the night
secluded
erotic
forgotten
with new friends forgotten in the brilliance of day
free in night's dampness
the lone embrace
when fog meet the moon
no longer neglected or pitied
down by the bridge
jubilation
new youth only drunkenness knows,
when fog greets the moon
where night's dampness sinks forgotten
on autumn's first night.

Sepia

Memories like old photographs exposed to the sun
fade into sepia's dull orange glow,
then the chance to make them as we want
a hint, a highlight to features
fragile, forgotten, seeping into nothingness,
few chosen memories set in gold
or for others, the blackest nights remembered
like the poetry of youth,

etched deep in the furthest corners and gullies
valleys, recesses, nooks where a glimmer
of light bursts through to highlight the colour
strangled in hidden alleys at night
slowly finding voice in the sad hours
between darkness and day, uncontrolled,

beyond the rules of government and finance
time captured in the holes of night and shadowland
silhouette trees take over with night's light playing
what was invisible now in counterpoint
darkness altering other shapes
strangled, rigid, more real than full daylight
these promises of evenings and new mornings
where the orgasm of day flows in,

no holding back
the control, manipulation
dreams sad, lost in the explosion, expansion
grasping longer futile
for daylight will come in the orchestra of dawn
leaving wrinkled night to the past.

Dubrovnik

Fleeting memories
behind yellowed ochre walls
lavender morning

Towards dawn

Evening's night is so black in regions far and remote
blacker than velvet
with its sequins of silver
stars claim new meaning,
new distances and horizons
where a late evening light cannot dim the ebony of night
darkest in regions unknown
unnamed in mountains
and deserts where camp fires
remain unheeded
as men gaze to stars
their companions and leaders to where sight cannot go.

Morning welcomes in the silver lacework filigree
of early dawn light
rays thin and soft
for the melding
patterns never the same twice over
promising light where dull heaviness
proclaimed and ruled
only hours before
in wastelands of sleeplessness
insomnia's control
gone as light breaks through
day's companion promising relief.

Fishing boats

Waves
smack gently
against wooden barques
making ready their morning
journey beyond the coastal town
where children will play on sunrise
sunlight not yet fully matured this dawn.
Fishermen and boys old enough murmuring early greetings
to neighbours checking rolled nets and tackle
baskets and oars as did fathers
before them long years before
ways unchanging at dawn
where time allows
slow morning
greetings.

Smoke

A smell of smoke awakens dreams' memories
crouching in deepest valleys of a mind
caught up in the fury of yesterday
a morning glad that the night has passed
though twisted again in the earliest hours
after daybreak
when smoke lingers in villages
oozing in beneath cracks
under doors
through ill-fitting windows
and minds unsealed
open enough
to grasp the sounds and invisible greyness
of smoke haze from a garden nearby
creeping through walls
too thin for the night
slinking and sidling
determined to wake.

Daybreak on Dubrovnik

Crates
unpacked and flagstones swept clean of last night's revelries
aluminium cans, ice cream wrappers and pizza boxes
taken for companionship down on the pier
after boats along the coast had ceased journeying
back and forth across the sea hugging rugged outcrops
coastline with memories longer than renovated market places
and the square in the old city made new,
far along the coast a hotel playground for the party
stands abandoned, forlorn, graffitied for boats to gaze on
and away, forgetting elites play on
in all situations.

Grand
entry through city gates, into secluded alleys
and squares set up as ice-cream stands and coffee houses
made ready for the new onslaught,
while travellers sleep on alongside burgers and old families
and clerics too old or disillusioned for prayers,
workers in the market place staggering silently
around the silent stones
glad of the peace in the city sleeping still,
slumbering as if yesterday
never happened.

Gone
signs of war and simmering feuds
aside from the photo display
mandatory on the street where old houses burnt
shell holes still visible for casual onlookers
held horror for families centuries within,
shocked that attack could happen from within and without
visitors later suitably tut-tutting
concerned, rebuking, murmuring complaint
but no more.

Days
few then gone again from memories most want to forget
on this morning with the light breaking through
yellow ramparts, fresh bulwarks, new fortifications
if ever a fresh onslaught, coming in
with income, outsiders with wealth from Europe
disappointment that unity has brought its own dilemmas
no longer outgoing but dreaming of a dream lost
to the dawn.

Dawn in the old city

Last night's thundering has subsided down on the waterfront
waves crashing against walls worn smooth again
after war's fury,
ramparts and pavements swept clean for visitors
interested in the romance of history today,
discreet, disinterested, unaware
of bruises and wounds still open and raw
turning away from it like neighbours turned away
from others growing alongside
where red geraniums grew
with the pink oleander hanging over walls
made bare in smoke
burnt without friendship
ripped out
as the sweeper this morning tears out cautious weeds
daring to shoot through cracks
in the battlements brittle in the sun
yellow as skeletons never were,
herbs hidden by weeds
collected for old women who still know the way
for visitors' fine fascination in their promises of fecundity
fertility still famous
in the land where the grapevines and olive groves
lie forgotten.

Fleeting images

Solitary hare
at the edge of a gold wheat field
sweetened at daybreak,
rejoicing its freedom
in changing shadows
while overhead blackbirds
sing, alerting the morning
turning silver in sunlight.

Dawn haiku

early sunshine snatches
grey skies promising relief
raining cornflowers

listening at sunrise
catching music in the wind
harmony promised

morning melody
transformed by strident chanting
seeking harmony

airwaves morning song
overtaken by chirping
drowning harmony

Mostar

sunrise rays on bridge
black slate lost under grey frost
claiming evening's sleep

Sunset on Mostar

She hastened to the place so public it was private enough,
to a crooked stone bridge across the river
down near an old tinsmith forge
long since closed down,
as red rays of sunset seeped in down laneways
bursting across and down the river
the rippling glow
soon ablaze with fire.

Others trudged towards her and beyond,
some hurrying in light's exuberance
fading too soon
at the end of these days in late summer,
crimson orange promises
shot with passion of gold
twisting for those short summer seconds
as the sun came down.

Evening

She stood alone of the edge of Stari Most bridge
enveloped by the soft sounds
of calm early evening
waiting for the promise that again they would meet
capturing once more scents fleetingly held
alluring
enticing
at the end of the day.

Lights reflecting from an old cobbled building
further along
where the road met a wooden boat landing
her sole companion
as her heart sank with the sun
rising to wild song's crescendo
as footsteps approached
promising music with early evening's glow.

Night

She shivered in the starkness of night
throwing off day's mantle of warmth
with the serenade
of silent evening
seducing her further into danger
and darkness's dreaming,
the place with its mists
where nightmares begin.

Yesterday's meeting and its final chance
promising escape
and unknown relief
from sameness to freedom
waning pledges
of protection for vassals of the state
disappearing in the night
as the sun finally came down over Mostar.

Daybreak

She crept out with the early rays of dawn
to the place on the bridge
where they had promised to meet,
the sound of morning grey turtle doves
lifting her spirits
where moments before only dark shadows lurked
there on the bridge
alone near nets piled high the previous night,

before she had learnt
and before the sun had come down
before the singing changed from fiddle to drum
thumping wildly as street boys
settled into alcoves
subsiding to dull drumming
drowned by late summer crickets
claiming rule of the night.

Cold chased afar by rays of the morning
again dawning yellow and gold
melting the ice of her fear
meetings promised and promises at meeting
no longer mattered
on that young autumn morning
where the sun had come up
over freedom's bridge.

www.ingramcontent.com/pod-product-compliance
Lightning Source LLC
Chambersburg PA
CBHW070942080526
44589CB00013B/1615